DORIS DINGLE'S
CRAFTY CAT
ACTIVITY BOOK

DORIS DINGLE'S CRAFTY CAT ACTIVITY BOOK

Games, Toys & Hobbies
to Keep Your Cat's Mind Active

Written by
Helen Levchuk

Illustrated by
John Bianchi

Alaska Northwest Books™
Anchorage · Seattle

Published in Canada by
Douglas & McIntyre Ltd., 1990

Library of Congress Cataloging-in-Publication Data
Levchuk, Helen.
    Doris Dingle's crafty cat activity book : games, toys and
hobbies to keep your cat's mind active / written by Helen
Levchuk ; illustrated by John Bianchi.
        p.   cm.
    ISBN 0-88240-415-6
    1. Games for cats.   2. Toys for cats.   3. Toy making.
4. Cats—Humor.   I. Title.
SF446.7.L48   1991
636.8'088'7—dc20   91-2701
                                                        CIP

Editorial and design by Abraham Tanaka Associates

Printed and bound in Singapore

Alaska Northwest Books™
A division of GTE Discovery Publications, Inc.
22026 20th Avenue S.E.
Bothell, Washington 98021

To my dear sister and friend, Carole.
H.L.

With special thanks to Peggy Dowell, D.V.M.

CONTENTS

3 Catnip / 51

4 Toys & Stuff / 56

INTRODUCTION

Hello, fellow cat lovers,

First off, let me thank you for buying my book. It's not cheap, so already I know you must love your cat a lot. And why shouldn't you? Cats are wonderful and well deserving of love and admiration.

I have had a cat ever since I had my first home. That was a long time back when I was very young and got married, as all nice church girls did back then. Only trouble was, I loved my cat — a big black, gentle, long-haired stray named Sylvia — more than the Kingpin. He said I was like a cat — proud, independent; sometimes recklessly gay & social, sometimes brooding & inward. (He preferred dogs — dripping humility, but most of all, obedient.) So with my cat and knitting needles under my arm, I decided to have enough sense and dignity to save my life by ending my marriage.

And what a life it has been, with a great deal of thanks going to dear hearts like Sylvia, Sheba, Gypsy and Pippin (God rest their sweet souls), and my current crew — Donna, Dayoh, Dee Dee, Cia, and the zany Siamese sisters, Sheena & Bambi.

Lordy, lordy, how much I've learned from my precious furry friends, and how much less worldly wise I'd be without these insights, which I attempt to apply to my life with typically human clumsiness. Things like sitting very still (people are very poor at this) and letting the mind drift off to alpha, or silently examining a ladybug on a leaf, or all the other small & great things that go unnoticed as we scurry through life.

The cats and I live in a big, rickety-rackety old house that badly needs to be undecorated.

We are working on this ourselves, as we can hardly pay our bills, let alone decorators! Cia, Dayoh and the kittens have ripped off most of the wallpaper on the lower parts of the walls, though I'm really getting behind on the top parts because of my arthritis. The place is a real mess, and my sister Pearl, who sometimes helps, says we should concentrate on one area at a time. But the cats & I would rather enjoy ourselves, as we know we're incapable of being organized.

Every cat I have known and loved has known and loved me even better. I'm even fond of old strays that I stop and chat with on my way to the post office. Some people in town think I'm droll and daft, but most just think of me as the lady who loves cats.

I keep telling people I'm not an expert on cats, but I won't deny I know a heck of a lot. God knows I do ramble on about them, and people always seem to be interested in my advice, so finally I decided to share what I know to be true from my own observations and experiences and write some of it down in a book of toys and games. I know for sure, the loving act of playfulness can perk up life for you and your cat and warm you right to the end of your nose and the tips of your toes.

All the toys and games in this book have been thoroughly tested by my little furry friends to get out the bugs. I hope you read every page of my book, enjoy it and use it, as already I know it can change dullness into delight for you and your cat.

There is no sweeter love-gift than a hand-made toy. There is no greater fun than sharing a good game with a pal.

Yours with hugs,

Doris Dingle

1
GAMES

Loving and caring for your cat is one thing. Having a fantastic relationship with your cat is something else. You can bet your cat knows every last thing about you, even though he or she may not be that affectionate or show much interest in anything other than your maid services. Just like with people, friendships with cats start from scratch and grow through sharing and caring, through good times and bad.

It's up to you to start the relationship by having regular & loving conversations with your cat. You can talk about anything—your day at the office, your love life, your plans for a new deck, your fear of thunder & lightning. Kitty is always there for you, and your secrets are safe. One warning, though. Cats can read minds, so you'd better be careful not to get *too* depressed, or puss will start to worry.

To round out a perfect friendship, there must also be times for fun & games. I would like to share with you some of the games I've played with my cats over many, many years. Not all cats will like all games, but I'm sure there are lots your puss will be crazy about.

Firstly, the better you know your cat, the easier it will be to choose the right games. Or, what the heck, try them all! But do consider your cat's age. Wild & woolly kittens will play at almost anything til they drop. Some older cats are set in their ways and like to specialize in one or two activities, just like people who've gotten hooked on tennis or darts but wouldn't be caught dead bowling or scuba-diving.

Also consider whether your cat is in the mood for play. Don't wake puss from a nap or daydreaming and say, "Come on, Mixmeister, into the tub for a game of jai alai!" Wait

til he is wandering around looking for something to do and then let the games begin!

Don't give up on a game too soon. Give your cat some time to get the hang of it. If there is no interest, try again on another day. Hey, I don't have to tell you, it's just like with us—some days we'd rather go roller-skating and some days we'd rather play bingo or watch the soaps. And that's what makes life so interesting, whether you're a person or a cat.

FOILBALL-OFF-THE-WALL

This game is best played on stairs. I thought Dayoh and I had invented it, but what do I find? My friend Billy Chong has been playing it for years with his cats, Mallorey and Opie.

WHAT YOU NEED

- Foilball (you get a piece of cooking foil about the size of a dinner napkin and mush it up into a tight ball).
- Stairs with backs and a wall on one side and rungs on the other (so puss doesn't fall and break his neck).

HOW TO PLAY

If your cat has never seen a foilball before, let him get used to it. Give it a little toss so it cathum-cathum-cathums across the linoleum, making a jolly-rolly sound. Your cat will love it. Let him bat the foilball around so he gets the feel & smell of it. Better yet, make a few balls the day before and just let them hang around.

Put puss near the top of the stairs, maybe two or three steps from the top. You go to the bottom of the stairs and, aiming carefully, give the foilball a good fling against the wall, about two steps in front of where your dearie is sitting. Either he'll go after the ball or he won't (then you'll have to take a few more shots). Some cats who have never seen anything like this before will just be amazed and sit & watch while you have all the fun.

Once kitty starts playing, you can just spectate til the ball bounces to the bottom. Then it's up to you to fling it against the wall again. When flinging, always aim behind kitty when he's on the lower part of the stairs and in front of him when he's near the top. Otherwise he might turn too fast and end up with whiplash.

Sometimes Dayoh will carry the ball in his mouth to the top of the stairs and sit there looking down at me, just like King Farouk. He calls this game Make-Mammy-Climb-the-Stairs. He does this twice until I say, "No way, Jose," and go make myself a nice cup of tea.

For more fun and less climbing, play with two or three balls.

Three Blind Mice

What is life for a cat without a mousehole to peek into? This game has three. Open one, open two or open three, and let one or more curious cats try to catch the three blind mice who live inside.

What You Need

- Three big peanuts.
- Three nice pieces of yarn, each about 8 inches (20 cm) long.
- A darning needle.
- A nice firm cardboard box (with lid attached) about 4 to 6 inches (10 to 15 cm) square. (I think those mugs with funny sayings on them come in these, but mine is from a stoneware garlic keeper.)
- A couple of pinches of dried catnip.
- A felt pen (for drawing mouseholes).
- An X-acto knife (for cutting them out).

How to Make It

To make the mouse house, trace a mousehole pattern on three different sides of the box. With the X-acto knife, carefully cut around the arches of the mousehole, but not across the bottom. Pull the holes open and look inside. Isn't it cozy in there? Shut them up again.

NICE CATHEDRAL-STYLE MOUSEHOLE PATTERN

Now thread a piece of yarn through the darning needle and make a nice big knot at the end. Gently push the needle longways from one end of the peanut to the other. Pull the needle through. That's it! Now you've got a mouse with a cute nose & tail but no eyes. If you like eyes, draw them on, but I wouldn't bother. If the peanut breaks, eat it and try again with a fresh one.

Make three of these little critters and throw them in their house with a pinch or two of catnip. Close the lid on the mouse house.

HOW TO PLAY

All you have to do is sit the game in front of kitty, then open one of the holes, or maybe even two or three. If your furry friend gives you a chance, have another peek inside for a cat's-eye-view of the light shining through on those three mice sitting in catnip. Isn't it a wonderful sight?

Now get out of the way and let pussums have her fun getting out the mice and then the catnip. When the game finishes, close the mouseholes, open the top and throw the escaped mice back in. Put the game away in your cat's toy box for next time. If a few days go by, it would be nice to freshen up the catnip before the next game.

SHOEBOX RIDE

This can be casual, scenic, thrilly, topsy-turvy or even Evel Knievel. It all depends on what your cat is into. But even if puss is a daredevil, it's best to start slow, or you might put him off. This would be a bummer, as this game is first-rate.

WHAT YOU NEED

- A shoebox (or boot box if your cat is plump like my Dayoh).
- A piece of good strong string or yarn — at least 3 feet (1 m) but better longer.
- A knitting needle or skewer to poke a hole in the box.

HOW TO MAKE IT

With the knitting needle, poke a hole in the middle of the end of the shoebox. Insert the string and tie a very strong knot. That's it! All aboard!

HOW TO PLAY

As with all new games, your cat will want to thoroughly check out the equipment first — sniff the Tender Tootsie's box, try it for fit, push to see if anything's under it, chew the string, etc. After the inspection is complete and kitty is comfortable with this strange contraption, give the box a slow dry run so puss can figure out what it's for. Maybe she'll walk around behind it. Maybe she'll jump inside. Maybe she'll just sit there with a lot of ??????'s above her head. Maybe you'll have to put her inside. Let her sit before you pull, and then go very slowly til she looks like she's having a good time. Speed up a bit, but don't try anything fancy til the second or third ride.

VARIATIONS

Smooth-rug ride: This is almost a wimpy ride, as all you do is pull puss round & round on a big rug or broadloom. Seniors like it, and it's a good way to start. It can get boring for you awfully fast and also produce dizziness. In either case, go to a figure eight pattern to get undizzed.

Lumpy-rug ride: This is more fun. Put a few folds in the rug to make some upsy-downsies. My cats love hiding things under the rugs, and these are extra tush-ticklers. Do you think they care that I could sprain my ankle stepping on a walnut or a biff bag? Not a whisker!

Floor ride: This is like the rug ride only noisier, as the box screeches over all the nernies on your linoleum. Wood floors are also nice & noisy. The grittier your floor, the greater the ambiance.

All-around-the-house ride: This is like your tour bus ride, hitting all the high spots in the home. I like to announce points of special interest ("Here's the lazy-boy chair Donna destroyed. These are the drapes Sheena & Bambi swing from. Up there's where I hide the catnip."). Pull the box under the coffee table and say it's the Holland Tunnel. Cats love folks with a good sense of humor.

Round-&-round ride: This is sort of like sitting in the swan on the merry-go-round. Don't make the ride too long, or kitty will get dizzy, but you can go fast if he likes speed. You stand in an open area and pull the box around you in a circle, passing the string from hand to hand to keep it going.

Tipsy ride: This is like reckless driving — very fast — and you end up crashing or being thrown from the vehicle. The kittens love it, but most mature cats will find it stupid. If your cat is into raucous activities like my little cross-eyed twins are, start this ride at a good pace and speed up as you race through the house. Often kitty will wipe out on the turns, but with practice he'll learn to hang on and lean for balance.

Big Box O' Balls

This is absolutely my favorite game to play with my dearies. Everyone joins in, either as a player or a hip spectator. Bambi loves fetching paperballs, so sometimes I just have to sit there with my brewskie and be the sharp-shooter.

What You Need

- A big cardboard fruit box (with top) from the supermarket. Try to get one with peep holes in the side. Avoid ones that are moldy or otherwise scuzzy.
- A whole lot of paperballs—twenty, thirty, forty or more. You make these from useless paper that would just go to waste, like memos from the boss (always remove staples), junk mail (including envelopes), small paper bags, Book-of-the-Month Club inserts—anything that's a decent-quality paper (no newsprint) that will scrunch up into a nice ball that holds its shape. A variety of weights & sizes & colors makes the game more interesting. You can keep adding balls as you go til it's just right.

How to Play

Cats are plum crazy about both boxes & paper-balls, so they'll already be playing while you're still rolling up the balls.

To officially play, you put the bottom part of the box with the peepholes in a good open spot and park yourself on the floor opposite it with the lid of the box filled with balls—how far you sit from the box depends on how good a shot you are.

What you do is shoot the paperballs into the box, which is hunky-dory all on its own. But with your little pal participating, it's a real hoot, as he'll be playing his own game, which could be any of the following:

- Sit in front of the box and intercept the paper-ball before it gets in (this is usually played on long arching shots).
- Sit inside the box and wait for incoming balls (sometimes puss will try to stop them; sometimes he'll want to see how many times you can hit him on the head).
- Roll around inside the box o' balls waiting for UFO's to land on him.

When this turns into a multi-cat game, anything can happen, depending on whether the cats want to play as a team or every cat for himself. Sometimes I keep score on the side of the box, just for the record.

To start a new game, just dump the balls from the bottom into the top, and there you go. (When your boyfriend or the church ladies come over and you want to cuten-up the place, just shove the BBOB's under your bed.)

CORK-ON-A-ROPE

With cork-on-a-rope you & puss can play many games. Or you can just spectate while puss plays on her own.

Everything about corks is perfect for cat toys. They're light, pliable, sound good — and they come free on top of your nice bottles of wine.

WHAT YOU NEED

- A wooden spoon or a short, strong, attractive tree branch.
- One wine cork.
- A darning needle.
- A pair of pliers.
- A long piece of string or yarn, about 6 to 9 feet (2 to 3 m) long (suit yourself).

HOW TO MAKE IT

Thread the needle with the string and run the needle through the length of the cork. When the nose of the needle pokes through, use pliers to pull it clear. Tie the end of the string around the cork.

Tie the other end of the string around the handle of the spoon or branch and wind it around to keep the toy neat til playtime.

DRAGSY

Around the house we go, jogging in time to some nice polka music. Up & down the stairs, with the kits hopping & whirling after the bouncing cork-on-a-rope.

BATSY

You hold up the toy so the cork dangles an arm's length (cat's arm) above puss's nose. She bats at it — thwack! thwack! And when it hits her in the head, it doesn't hurt.

JUMPSY

Like Batsy, but you hold the cork up higher and let puss jump for it. My Siamese girls love this game and shoot straight up from the floor like little furry missiles.

LAZY

Watch your soaps and play with the cats at the same time. You just throw out the cork the full length of the string and start reeling it in at your leisure. You can fool kitty by reeling it back in as he carries the cork away in his mouth til . . . whoops! When the commercials are on, reel in the cork close to your chair so kit can play Batsy or Jumpsy for a while and shred the side of your chair if she hasn't done so already.

KIT PLAYS ALONE

When you're busy painting your fingernails or heavily into your Barbara Cartland novel or have to go out for groceries, you can set up the game so puss can play alone. It's easy. Adjust the string to the right length so it hangs above kit's nose and secure the wooden spoon in a vertical position in a drawer or tuck it down the side of a chair cushion so the string can't unwind.

DIZZY

You hold the toy above puss's head and swing it either back & forth or round & round, or combine both moves til you can tell by the look on her face that she's starting to see stars.

Bathtub Jai Alai

This is a heck of a great game!! I've never known a cat who didn't love it. Even seniors can have a wonderful time, as they can play at their own level.

What You Need

- One small — 1- to 1 1/2-inch (2.5 to 4 cm) — hard rubber ball sold at variety and five-and-dime stores.

How to Play

Wash the bathtub out real good and be sure to rinse, too, as Comet between the toes is hell to lick out. Next, dry the tub, or you might put kitty off his game. Then put the bathtub plug in the hole so the ball won't get caught in there. Remove shampoo bottles, bubble bath, etc., from the sides of the tub.

Put your wee sport in the nice clean tub, and if it's his first time, let him get used to the place. Talk to him in a happy voice and chuck him under the chin so he knows something special is going to happen.

Show kitty the ball and say "Jai alai!" Then give the ball a gentle roll up the side of the tub. Puss will know exactly what to do from there. Your fun is to sit at the end of the tub near the plug and keep the ball in play. With some cats you won't need to do anything more than be a spectator and cheer. Others like the added things you can do, like bouncing the ball off the sides and around the plug area. So suit yourself, but I'll bet you'll want to play. If you have more than one cat, try a game of doubles. If you have a whole lot, provide good seats for spectators, or else they'll jump into the tub and you could have a rumble on your hands.

FETCH

Cats have too high a regard for themselves to become the students of people. For this alone they deserve our respect and admiration. So I'm not going to tell you that you can teach your cat to fetch. It's really up to puss to decide when, what and if she wants to fetch. I'm sure all cats *can* fetch if they choose to do so, so they may all enjoy this game once they have developed a relationship with their tall two-legged friends.

Here are some of the things cats find fetchable:

- Paperballs are tops! Bambi fetches them, and so do her beautiful tortie-point mom and chocolate-point grandma.
- Foilballs (see page 14). These are Dayoh's fave, followed by pipecleaner pretzels (see page 75). Many of my friends' cats like foilballs, too.
- Bitsy sock balls. I used to cut these dumb balls off the backs of tennis socks, and Donna took to collecting & fetching them.
- Rabbits' feet. DeeDee got one for a gift many years ago. She loved it & washed it & took it to bed like it was her baby. She would carry it to my feet and drop it, and the fetch game would begin.

- Biff bags (see page 78). Many years ago my sister Pearl's neighbor and her fetching calico, Tyke, introduced me to biff bags.
- Anything goes. Some cats will fetch *anything*. I know one amazing cat who would try to drag back a chair if you threw it across the room.

Many cats prefer a more creative version of Fetch — they bring you whatever they want . . . whenever they want. Here are some extra-special gifts my loved ones have fetched for me:

- My first cat, Sylvia, brought me a mouton collar she'd spotted in someone's trash can.
- Many cats will honor you with the most magnificent of gifts — a bird. Gypsy was never into bird-catching, but one day she dragged home a dead pigeon from St. Tim's church and presented it to me.
- Dayoh is the most generous and innovative gift-giver. He has presented me with numerous garter snakes, mice and grasshoppers, which he first arranges attractively in front of the patio doors, and once he brought home some home-fried potatoes with ketchup that my neighbor Mary had put out for the birds.

WATER GAMES & SPORTS

People who think cats don't like water have a very underdeveloped understanding of our fascinating feline friends. The thing is, cats like water as they choose, not as we would expect, which is totally in keeping with their interesting and independent characters.

Over the years my cats have turned up their collective hooters at every water game I ever made for them. These they came up with on their own.

BOBBING FOR PRODUCE

Forget the beautiful floating cork games with sailboats and sharks that I made for them. My kits would rather bat & dive for floating cauliflower, broccoli, green beans, romaine. Their absolute favorite is floating cucumbers being soaked for pickling.

Let them eat what they catch. Veggies are good for cats.

WATER CATCHING

A dripping or slowly running faucet is all it takes to get puss playing this dumb game he never wins, but never gives up on. My cats start by trying to catch the water by hand, which is impossible, no matter how hard they

try. Next they try their versatile, carry-all mouths, resulting in assorted gagging, sneezing & hiffting (water up hooter). The bathroom is best suited for this game. If puss insists on playing in the kitchen sink, she just needs to fall into the dishwater once to be cured forever of this water-catching location.

WATER CHASING

This game is great fun, not only for DeeDee & the little girls, but me, too.

When I'm out watering with the hose, I take off the spray nozzle and let the water cascade out, moving it from one plant to the next. As far as I can figure, the point of the game is to get a good swat at the water while trying to stay as dry as possible.

No matter how hard I try to keep from splashing the girls, who take up positions behind different plants, they always seem to zig when they should zag or attack when they should retreat. Even when they're soaked & spattered with mud, they'll keep hopping & pouncing & batting at the water. Maybe the point of this game is really to get as grubby as possible!

RUN-THRU-THE-SPRINKLER

When we were little girls, my sister & I used to play this game on our back lawn. Now my rambunctious Siamese sisters especially delight in this water sport, but the older cats just watch them and walk around the sprinkler like responsible adults.

The kittens prefer the little plastic sprinkler that goes round & round. They start by chasing the water in circles for two or three laps, stopping dead, then making a mad dash through the middle. They hardly get wet, except for their feet, right up to their knees.

It is important to keep the water pressure low enough so the sprinkler doesn't go around at breakneck speed.

Forget this game if your cats are past kittenhood. They may well have liked this sport back then, but already it's too late, unless they're slightly goofy.

Bubble Games

How sweet it is to go out in the yard with your dear kits on a nice day when there's a bit of a breeze and blow them a yardful of sparkling, drifting, dancing bubbles.

Donna, DeeDee, and even cool dude Dayoh and the wild little twins are amazed & enchanted by the wonder of bubbles. The older cats watch them & smile, just like parents at their kid's dance recital. Sheena & Bambi, who attack everything that moves, follow the bubbles with their elegant brown noses in the air as if they're in a trance.

I'm sure if cats could blow with their mouths like us, they'd pucker up their little leather lips and have bubble parties all the time. But then they'd likely go on to learn how to whistle, which would be more than even a patient person like myself could handle.

You can buy bubble soap for your guys & gals where toys are sold. It comes with a blower or two. After you use it all up, be thrifty and make your own by mixing 1/2 cup (125 mL) water with 2 tablespoons (25 mL) dishwashing liquid.*

You can even make your own blower by bending a length of copper or brass wire into a shape like this:

I made mine out of brass, and it is not only beautiful, but because of the nice big circle, it makes bigger bubbles than the chintzy little plastic ones that come with the bought stuff.

Sometimes on sunny winter days I mix up a batch of bubble soap, and as those magical orbs float around the kitchen, the cats & I dream of summer & butterflies cruising through our catnip patch.

---

* Some brands work better than others, so if your brand is not making bubbles the size of small grapefruits, borrow another brand from your neighbor. The secret of good, big bubbles is to hold your mouth close to the blower and blow very gently. Then flip the big bubble off with a flick of your wrist.

BALLOON GAMES

Balloon games are not for cats or people with bad nerves, as every game ends with a bang. I like playing with round balloons, which bounce & roll better than the weenie shapes.

All on its own, a balloon is a terrific toy, and puss will make up many games without your help. Even a broken balloon* is a hoot for a cat to carry around, attack, fling, nip at or hide under the chesterfield. Bambi likes to hold one end down with her foot and pull the other with her mouth til it snaps her on the nose. Why she likes this is beyond me.

The best way to get ready for balloon games is to blow one up—not too full or it will pop more easily (especially on a hot day). Toss the balloon on the floor and let kitty get the feel & smell of it. Games work better if kitty is balloon-wise to begin with.

BAT THE BALLOON

This is the gentlest of games. You & puss take turns batting the balloon as it bounces off a wall. It is played either sitting on the floor or, better yet, when there is a sofa in front of the wall. With puss sitting on the sofa and you on the floor, you are both pretty much at the

* Cats love chewing rubber, so don't leave puss on her own with a broken balloon, or she might swallow it.

same height to bat the balloon as it comes off the wall.

The kittens like playing this game on the stairs, as they're wild & crazy girls. Bambi is an excellent batter, and I think Sheena gets a bit jealous, as she often bites the balloon to end the game.

HIDE THE BALLOON

This game is too silly for grown-up cats to take seriously, but the kittens think it's far out. Their big brother & sisters always give me dirty looks when I play it, as it tends to make the little girls crazier than usual.

The game is played simply by hiding a blown-up balloon under something, which forms an unusual lump in an unusual place. First off, the kittens inspect it, then bat at it to make an enchanting squeaky-rubber sound, then attack it to make a big bang. This is a perfect excuse to flash their bottle-brush tails and run up the drapes.

Here are some good places to hide balloons: under rugs, mats, afghans, blankets, towels and, my most favorite of all, in my sweatshirt or trackpants while I'm wearing them!

BEACHBALL GAMES

You don't have to take your little fur friends to the seashore to have fun playing beachball games. Your own backyard will do just fine, as will a big room in your house, or a nice big space in your apartment.

Most every cat likes playing beachball games, but every cat has his own idea of what's fun & what's not. Thank heavens there are more than enough games to please everyone!

Before you try to play anything, let puss get used to the feel and smell of this giant plastic monster, as at first impression it will likely be very scary. Let the ball just hang around the house for a day or two. Now & then, give it a little tap with your foot so kitty can see how harmless it is and how gently it moves around without hardly making a sound. Before you know it, puss himself will be batting it around, trying to tempt you to leave your chores and join in the fun.

Here are some games you & your dearies might enjoy.

SOCK IT TO ME

Bounce the ball right off kitty's noggin. Gypsy & Pippin just loved this game, which started off as an accident and ended up as a big hit with this mild-mannered twosome.

The kittens, who are real show-offs, like to volley the ball back. Make sure the cats & you are more or less at the same level—for example, with them on a dresser, bookcase or table — or wait til you're both loitering on the chesterfield.

Macho man Dayoh absolutely hates this game. I think this is because he watched the TV reruns of The Prisoner, which greatly disturbed him.

SOCCER

This is an outdoor game, though you could play it in your rec room if it's big enough. It is also one of those "more-the-merrier" games where all the cats and the whole family can join in, depending on the size of your playing field.

Family tots should be spectators only, as they tend to kick the cats more than the ball and often do that piercing, over-excited screaming that makes everyone's hair stand on end. But if your kids are cool, they can have as much fun as the cats.

The beachball is put into play by kicking it with the instep of your foot toward one of the cats or other players.

Rules: Players who stand on their hind legs cannot touch the ball with their hands (except to put it into play), but rather must try to keep it moving, preferably through the air, with their feet. End of rules.

The cats can use both hands & feet, as they prefer to jump at the ball in the air and then run off to take a position for their next attack. Some cats like Dayoh are good at moving the ball along the ground, so if yours is thus inclined, be sure not to kick him as you try to intercept the ball.

There is no scoring, since this game is just an excuse to romp around and maybe get a little exercise. Afterwards, my sister Pearl & I usually relax under the mulberry tree with a couple of Lite ones.

BIG BALL IN A BIG BAG

Of all the wild & woolly games we play, this one is absolutely the most reckless and to our liking. But before you start the game, you might want to move the family heirlooms to a safe place, because if your kits play like mine do, you'll think a tornado is going through the house.

For you, this game is as easy as setting it up, then sitting back to spectate. What you do is put your beachball into a big hard-plastic garbage bag like those brown industrial-strength ones. Leave the end of the bag open so your wee minx will crawl in to explore, creating a crinkly racket with every step she takes. What puss does in there is beyond me, but it sure is raucous and seems like something I could enjoy if I were smaller. One cat's clattering will make all the cats come running, and then things can start getting hairy. Sometimes outside cats will pounce on inside cats, or sometimes they, too, will crawl inside. Before you know it, you've got a clamoring bag of cats rolling across the floor. (If you really want to be a devil, toss a few cat yummies or a spoonful or so of catnip into the bag.)

FATCAT BALL

This is a gentle game for elderly and/or crotch-ety cats. My big muffy Cia is getting on in years (but aren't we all). Then, too, she's a bit on the heavy side and, to put it kindly, a moody type. On good days, she's not quite as lighthearted as Queen Victoria in her latter years. On bad days, she's like Orca, killer whale. Even my neighbor Mr. Gonzo is respectful of her awesome persona.

Here is a beachball game I came up with especially for Cia. If you have a puss who is past her prime, she might enjoy it, too.

Wait til puss is lying on the floor, just lounging around in a very relaxed mode. Sit down on the floor a short distance away from her and gently roll the beachball toward her. Chances are she will bat it back, but if she doesn't, don't give up too easily, as these types of cats often are not over-anxious to get involved in new experiences.

Cia plays this game with her front feet and her supreme hindquarters, every now & then unsuccessfully trying to get her death-grip on the friendly plastic and muttering feline swear words. That's just how she is; who knows how impossible we might be when we get to be her age!

Fuzzy Dollies' Beauty & Massage Parlor

I've always made a game of grooming my little ones, which is a whole lot better than making a chore of it. My sister Pearl laughs at me and says I'm like a big kid playing with my fuzzy dollies. How right she is, as this is a happy time when I get to admire every last hair of my beauties individually. Sometimes they tip me with little kisses & love-bites and hum sweet songs while I work on them.

Each cat has a weekly appointment that I set up at my convenience, not theirs, so sometimes they complain just like people. If you have more than one cat, try to do them one after another; otherwise there could be a bit of jealousy.

As I don't have to tell you, cats by nature are very clean and proud of their good looks, and they spend a lot of time each day on grooming. But they will still appreciate the extra attention you can give them.

Start grooming early when your cats are kittens, so they will be easy to handle. Give special attention and services to senior citizens who may not be able to groom themselves as well as they used to, because of loss of flexibility, arthritis, etc.

While you are grooming your babies, check them over for any lumps or abscesses. This is particularly important if your cats go outdoors and get into rumbles. Often puncture wounds don't show up til they become abscessed, so the sooner you discover them, the sooner they can be treated.

When his appointment is over, give puss a couple of yummies for being so cooperative.

What You Need

- Your favorite perfume or cologne.
- Several cotton balls.
- A soft cat brush (Hartz makes a nice one).
- A fine-tooth metal comb (flea comb from the pet store).
- A small dish of warm water.
- Cotton swabs.
- Vegetable or mineral oil.
- Facial tissues.
- A chair with a small trash bag hanging from it.

Setting up Shop

Most of your job is done standing, so depending on how tall you are, choose a tabletop or countertop that's the right height for you. Make sure it has a washable surface, good light and ample space to set up your stuff.

Sing, hum, act jolly and make pleasant small talk (maybe steal a few lines from your own hairdresser) while you set up, so your sweethearts will pick up your good vibes and know something excellent is about to happen. After your dollies have their beauty treatment a few times, they'll start hopping up on the table or counter as soon as they see you getting ready.

When you're ready for your first client, spray both wrists with your favorite scent. Little by little this will rub off on your honey's beautiful fur coat, and by the time the beauty treatment is complete, kitty will have taken on a familiar fragrance you both love.

Nail Clipping

Assuming you've cut your cat's nails before, you know how it's done. If not, skip this step until you get instructions from your vet or one of the many fine cat care books at your library. I've found the best way to trim nails is with both puss and me in a sitting position—that is puss sitting on his back on my lap, with my left arm across his belly for a firm grip and my left hand free to press the pads under his claws so he'll eject them for inspection & trimming. (I learned this comfortable method on my own and not from a book, so I thought I shouldn't hoard such a discovery.)

Don't feel you have to cut every claw, as sometimes only one or two really need it. And most important of all, be happy, calm, talk sweetly and bend down & kiss puss right on his forehead now & then.

Eyes

At least once a day I check my cats' eyes for boogers and gently scrape them out with my thumbnail. At my salon I also add a wee wash of the eye area with a cotton ball dipped in warm water. Only do this if you see a bit of crustiness under the area of the eye duct. Otherwise, forget it.

Ears

As a rule, kitty does a fine job cleaning her own ears. Bambi & Sheena are also crazy about washing the ears of the other cats and often get a good slap from Cia or Dayoh for their trouble. However, it's always a good idea to check inside those perky ears to see what's going on in there. If the inside is nice and clean, just give puss a smooch on the forehead and maybe nibble her ears, which is very enjoyable for both parties, although I know you would never let Mr. Gino take such liberties with your ears. Unless he was really cute. Ha, ha, hairdressing humor.

If you spot a bit of wax or dirt, wrap one of your tissues around your index finger and stick it into the ear and gently rotate it. Use a fresh tissue for the other ear. If there's some dirt trapped in one of the folds, use a cotton swab dipped in water or vegetable oil. I know you wouldn't be dumb enough to shove the swab down kitty's eardrum hole, but just in case you're not too sure of what you're doing, play it safe by cleaning in the big folds only. If you see a lot of blackish-brown debris, poor puss may have ear mites, at which point you should call your vet.

BRUSHING & COMBING

Most cats love being brushed, and it's a real hands-on way of saying I love you. First-time brushers and brushees should concentrate on the easiest and most pleasurable areas like the top of the head, under the chin, the shoulders and back. After you and puss get the hang of the thing, don't be surprised to find her rolling over and asking you to do her belly hair. You'll get to know her favorite spots soon enough. Ideally, you should brush the whole body, but if puss gets persnickety about having something like her armpits brushed, sneak them in between her favorite spots. Keep cleaning the hair out of the brush into your hanging bag at the back of the chair.

If it's flea season and even one of your cats goes outdoors, run the fine metal flea comb through puss's fur and inspect for those nasty bloodsuckers. If there are fleas, they will get caught in the fine hair and fine teeth, so you should quickly drown them in a bowl of soapy water. At the first sign of even one flea, start a heavy-duty attack on them, or you and puss will pay dearly. Check with your vet or cat care books for the many methods and products available for dealing with these pests.

STYLING

When I backbrush DeeDee's long red ruff and crown hair, she is very pleased, as I think she considers herself a Princess Fergie lookalike, more or less.

Dayoh dotes on the fifties pompadour, styled by rolling and brushing his longish jet-black hair over my index finger, from the nape of his neck to the middle of his crown. He has a bit of a receding hairline, but with his handsome inky eyepatch he's still a heartthrob.

Cia, who is also long-haired, prefers an austere brushed-back look that suits her punctilious personality.

Short-haired cats like Gypsy & Pippin liked having their ruffs backbrushed a bit, creating a very foxy look when combined with a little finger-teasing of the hair above and below the chestbone until it formed a perfect ridge across the breast. This was particularly attractive on Pippin's trim Siamese body with its perfect tabby markings.

The kittens look awfully cute with the downy-chick do, which is done by pushing the crown hair back toward their noses with the thumb. A bit punkish, but okay for youngsters.

Fun & Games in Bed

Cats think of beds as more than nice places to grab a few zzzz's. Don't we all know that a cat has many beds and will sleep just about anywhere, from on top of the fridge to smack dab on your best church hat.

For my cats, my bed has always been considered something between a playing field and a fun house, complete with a lumpy body. I have no one to blame for this but myself, as I'm not inclined to say no-no to my pets' cavortings, but rather join in the sport.

Here are some tried-and-true bed games that are sure to please your fuzzy dollies and demolish your Springmaids.

Pillow Toss

This is sort of a watered-down version of the good old-fashioned pillow fight. What you do is toss your pillows, one at a time, right at old Maximillian. Won't he be surprised! After he finds out how great it feels to be bowled over by this friendly flying object, he'll insist that you toss him a few every morning when you make up the bed. This is a good way to be late for work.

Hills & Dales

The cats invented this game when I was nervy enough to ignore them and try to read in bed.

You make the hills & dales by getting under the covers and putting your knees up in a classic reading mode.

If puss has never clambered to the top of Mount Patella on his own, you might start by sitting him up there so he knows it's a cool thing to do. When he's comfortably smiling like the King of the Mountain, start spreading your knees apart to create a dale. Won't your little friend have a fit! Especially if you do it quickly, and he comes crashing down on your tummy. After he recovers, put your knees up again, and I'll bet he'll be right back up there waiting for the next quilt-quake to swallow him up.

My kittens love to leap to the top of the hill, and I often make my knees collapse just before they make contact. This baffles and bemuses them, which is a stimulating state to be in if you're a cat.

PUDDY IN A BLANKET

Cats adore being made up in the bed. Your morning chore can also be a great game for a funky feline who insists on lolling in the bed as you try to make it up.

What you do is make puddy up in the bed, piling the sheets and blankets and quilt on top of her (being sure you don't tuck her in so tight that she croaks).

When your little lump starts crawling around under the covers, give her a few oogah-boogahs on the back with your fingers to let her know you haven't abandoned her.

If your dearie has not found her way out after the bed is all made, pull up the coverlet to show her the way out. When she tumbles to the floor, pick her up and give her a big smooch, and have a nice day!

POUNCE

Every cat who has ever surveyed a bed with a lumpy person in it has played pounce. To make the game even more interesting, wiggle your toes under the covers. Your little guard cat will think some cheeky critter has invaded her secret domain and do her best to rout it out, starting with the critical pounce that announces detection, before the ultimate ferreting out.

I like to wiggle my fingers under the covers on one side and, when puss pounces, I fling the covers over her with my other hand, giving her a good tumble & tickling in the process. Kittens and rangy kits love this game. Seniors and proper pusses are not in the least amused by it.

Mother's Little Helpers

Cats are real homebodies and, as such, consider their homes to be their castles. No matter how grand or humble a cat's home may be, he will patrol, guard and love it with a passion. Don't you think we'd all be much happier people if we could love our own special places with such devotion?

Cats are so interested in every aspect of their homes that they are content to spend hours considering the pattern of the wallpaper, or the dripping of a faucet. Or, for all we know, they may be tuning in the action behind the wall or down the sewer line.

Is it any wonder, then, that your dear heart is incredibly interested in all your household activities and contraptions. Like curtains are for pulling back to let in the sunshine, but they are also excellent for climbing. The laundry basket is a cozy big boat that sometimes carries weird, exotic-smelling things on its trip to the laundry room and fresh, sweet-smelling ones on its trip back.

Whenever it's possible (and sometimes when it's not), I let my cats participate in my household chores and activities. Chores take longer, but never were they more fun!

Here are some everyday ho-hum household pastimes that you can turn into a romp for you and your little friends.

Laundry Sorting

Cats and kittens love dirty laundry, so I let my babies play to their hearts' content with my grungies.

I usually start by dumping the whole basket of dirty laundry on top of one of the cats. Don't be afraid. They love it. Then I begin sorting the laundry by tossing similar things into separate piles—whites with whites, sox & jeans, towels & terrys, etc. My cats usually station themselves on one of the piles, waiting to intercept incoming objects. Sometimes they just catch the flying sox or knickers, and sometimes they will take off with something they fancy. I may find this item many weeks later, under the chesterfield.

KITTY IN THE BASKET

Rightside up or upside down, your dearies will adore playing with the laundry basket. My cats lounge and roll inside the empty basket. Sometimes outsiders box at insiders through the bars. This basket-boxing works just as well with the basket upside down, so little brothers & sisters can bat at the caged kitties.

Baby Sheena is so strong, she drags the big plastic basket along the floor like a giant land turtle. Her sister usually jumps on top, stopping her in her tracks so that a boxing match can begin.

Sometimes I put one of the cats in the basket filled with clean laundry and carry him about like the Grand Poobah, lavishing him with praise. When I put the basket down, the other cats jump into the basket and have a good rumble while I put away the laundry.

SWEEPING & MOPPING

Have you ever noticed how cats like to be right in the path of your broom or mop when you're trying to cuten up the place? Maddening, isn't it? But there's nothing you can do about it, so just sweep Nosy Rosy right up with the dirt. Maybe she'll get the picture, but I doubt it.

WHOOPSY-DAISY

Even though cats get awfully embarrassed when they're caught in a clumsy act, they nevertheless enjoy playing Whoopsy-Daisy, one of the silliest games going.

All you have to do is try to pull the rug out from under old green eyes so he goes tumbling on his tush. "Whoopsy-daisy," you say, and if puss doesn't surrender the rug for shaking, you give him another whoopsy-daisy. Zany young cats, just like little kids, think falling down is great sport, but I wouldn't dare try this on a queen like Donna or a grump like Cia.

2
HOBBIES

Most cats have hobbies, though often we aren't even aware of them. But if your cat had to fill in her resume, you'd never hear the end of her interests & skills.

Here are some of the hobbies my cats enjoy. I hope they will encourage you to make hobby materials available for your clever cat's leisure hours.

It is very important to understand that cats are very proud of their work, so don't ignore it. Look at it! Admire it! Praise them! After a respectful period (minimum one day), hobby

& craft materials can be put into kitty's toy box for use at a later date.

BIRDWATCHING

There isn't a cat alive that doesn't enjoy bird-watching, and there are lots of things you can do to make this activity even more interesting for your birder.

THE SETUP

First, take inventory of all your windows. Look out of each (at your cat's eye level) and check out the view. Is it the side of your neighbor's ranch-style bungalow? Boring, boring, boring! Is it a tree or a bush? Wonderful! I guess you know which one to choose.

Now that you've picked your best bird-watching window, check out what's in front of it. Is it something good like a table or the back of a comfy chair or sofa? Perfect! Is it a big plant, a wooden chair or otherwise un-friendly object for a little fur tush? If so, start rearranging your furniture. Also make sure the piece of furniture doesn't have any wrong things on top of it, like your favorite vase. Another rule that's good to follow: keep plants to the rear of the viewing area or else kitty will have to rearrange them on her own, and sometimes she's a bit on the careless side.

If the viewing area is high, it's nice to provide a chair or something to help kit make it gracefully to the top without having to skid into your knick-knacks. Also remember to open the curtains or blinds before you go out, so kitty won't have to do it herself. If you have nosy neighbors, just a crack will do.

HERE, BIRDIE-BIRDIE

Now that everything's ready, what you need is birds, and that means a birdfeeder. There are all sorts of these that sit on poles or hang from trees or from the plant hooks where you hang your geraniums in the summer. Once the birds discover the chow, they'll come back all the time, so keep the feeder full. Also save all your scraps of bread, donuts, pizza crusts, crackers, etc., and just throw them on the ground. (I hate to nag but, unlike us, wee wild critters can't go to the Valu Mart, so we shouldn't be throwing perfectly good scraps into the landfill when hungry creatures can feast on them.) Cut-up apples and peanuts are popular with those silly squirrels that cats love to watch.

All the birds in my neighborhood know my cats intimately, as they share the same yard. The only time when problems occur is in late spring when baby birds, who are not cat-wise, sometimes fall prey to my beasties. So at this time of year I take extra care, making sure all the hunters (not all cats hunt) have miniature cowbells attached to their collars.

COLLECTING & ARRANGING

Dayoh is crazy about collecting and then arranging and rearranging his collections all over the house. He also sings while he collects & arranges, so I know he's really happy and proud of his work and not just doing it to prove he's artsy.

Dayoh's current favorite collection is wide elastic bands. Blue, green, red, yellow—these beauties come wrapped around broccoli. Wash them off with soap & water, rinse & dry them, and then throw them on the floor. Before you know it they'll be gone. Maybe your furry friend will just play with them. But if he's an artist, he'll arrange them in a nice row or pattern in the upstairs hall or right beside your bed, to show his high regard for you. (Don't ever give puss small narrow elastic bands no matter how pretty they are or how much he asks for them. They are no-no's as they can be swallowed, and poor puss could end up sick as a dog.)

Other good things for collecting are big plastic garbage bag ties, wine corks, foilballs, and odd pieces of ribbon (not metallic or string)—I tie these in neat little bows with

long tails—or anything else that's fun to carry around by mouth.

If you think you've come across something good, throw it on the floor. If it's still in the same spot the next day, throw it in the trash and think of something else.

READING THE NEWSPAPER

Cats aren't much for TV news, but they do enjoy reading the paper with you, particularly if you spread it out on the floor.

Most cats prefer to lounge as they read, just as we do, but they often do it on the exact story you're trying to peruse. Some cats can read the paper upside-down. Others want to read only what's of interest to them and will even crawl between the pages to get to their favorite sections. (If your cat walks on the paper, she's not really interested in what's going on in the world at all, but just wants attention.)

TV-Watching

Too much TV is not good for anyone, including cats. But a bit of good television never hurt anyone, so it's up to you to find out what your cat likes and then check the TV guide and turn the set on at the right time.

Here are the shows my cats like to watch:

Sports

Basketball is DeeDee & Dayoh's favorite sport. Next fave is hockey. Your cat might like something else, like tennis, but forget golf, baseball or curling.

Arts

I'm not sure whether my cats like opera or not, but they do like the singing, which is often similar to theirs. They're also crazy about the symphony, especially shots of the violin section.

But best of all is ballet. For my cats, the absolutely best ballet is the Kirov's Swan Lake. Donna sits right up close and moves her head from side to side when the corps de ballet flitters across the screen. I think I may get her the video.

Nature

If the subject is birds, insects or monkeys, the program will be a sure hit. Forget anything with dogs or dog-like creatures in it, especially if they yap or howl. DeeDee & Dayoh are terrified of werewolf howls, even when some silly comedian is doing his Count-Dracula-calling-his-dog-act.

Forget It

News, soaps, talk shows, rock videos or religious programs.

KNITTING

Can cats knit? You betcha! Donna's work is amazing. Sometimes she stays up half the night knitting. In the morning, what a surprise! A whole knitted living-room. Her major work was a two-level piece that started in an upstairs bedroom, went down the stairs, through the rungs, all around the living-room furniture, up the stairs, down the stairs, etc. I never figured out the pattern, but it was much more complicated and colorful than any Kaffe Fassett.

To get your cat started, find a nice box or basket and put it on the floor in a spot where it looks attractive. Fill it with balls of yarn. All colors. The more the merrier. Big balls, small balls, leftover balls. If you don't knit, ask friends who do to give you their leftovers. Stay away from anything fuzzy, like mohair, which will make puss gag. Look in the sale bins at your local department store for bargains. (But remember that new skeins of yarn must be rolled into balls.)

Once you've assembled the materials, your job is easy. All you do is admire your crafty kitty's handiwork. Then, after a while, roll up the balls and return them to their basket. A pair of scissors will come in handy on some of the heavy-duty tangles. Cats always enjoy watching people unknit. Sometimes they help. Sometimes they're a nuisance, but nobody's perfect.

3
CATNIP

Catnip, catmint, catnep—it's all the same wonderful stuff. Fresh, top-quality catnip is the be-all and end-all for funky feline activities. It's for sniffing, eating, drooling over, rolling in and likely for many other things we wouldn't even suspect. It is the odor rather than the flavor of catnip that excites cats from all walks of life—from strays to pillow puddings. Some breeders consider it an aphrodisiac and include it in mating rituals, along with soft lights and sweet music. For sure, it's a great source of vitamin C, and cats who ingest the leaves are likely getting a whole lot of other vitamins and minerals to put a spring in their step and a sparkle in their eye.

If you have a garden, catnip is easy as a weed to grow. And you'll need lots of it to make all the toys in Chapter 4.

To fully appreciate this remarkable plant, think of it in all its glory: fresh & flowering & fragrant—not the kind that comes in those dusty little boxes at the supermarket. I ask you, would you make yourself a cup of herbal tea from that stuff next to the pooper-scoopers? Not likely. But how about a nice cup of delicate catnip tea made from dried plants sold at the health food store, or better yet, from your own garden. Now we're talking!

Here are a couple of catnip teas for you & kitty to try.

CATNIP TEA FOR PEOPLE

Soothing for the stomach & nerves, it's sometimes called Mother Nature's Alka-Seltzer. I always let a little cool in the bottom of my cup for Bambi.

1 cup (250 mL) water
1 heaping spoonful dried catnip
1 heaping spoonful dried spearmint leaves
1 spoonful honey

Boil the water. Pour it over the mints and let it steep for 5 minutes. Strain it into a teacup and add the honey. Mm-mmm-mmm! So pleasant.

Maybe catnip is growing in your yard right now and you don't even know it. If you have something that looks and smells sort of like spearmint but has whiteish-pink flowers instead of purple, lucky you! Bruise a few leaves to release the oils & aroma and offer them to pudkins, and you'll know for sure. I've found catnip growing in the gardens of the last two houses we've moved in to, so check yours out and you might hit the jackpot.

CATNIP TEA FOR CATS

This was Gypsy's favorite, and baby Bambi likes it, too. The other kits couldn't care less about it, maybe because they don't like milk.

1 heaping spoonful dried catnip
1/2 cup (125 mL) boiling water
1/2 cup (125 mL) milk or cream

Steep the catnip in boiling water for 10 minutes, stirring several times. Strain it. Add milk and serve. Kitty will either purr your praises or look at you like you're nuts.

GROWING CATNIP

Catnip grows like a weed because it's not fussy. Any soil and location will do, even partial shade, though it loves the sun as much as your own dear puss. Just be sure to water it well until it becomes established.

Once your plants start flowering in July through September, they'll produce a lot of seeds, so you'll end up with more catnip plants than you'll know what to do with. Also remember that the plants are perennials, so they will come back in the spring after a nice winter snooze.

To get yourself started, you can buy seed from many seed supply stores. In Canada, you can order from Stokes Seeds Limited, Box 10, St. Catharines, Ontario, Canada L2R 6R6. In the United States, the address is Stokes Seeds Inc., Box 548, Buffalo, New York, U.S.A. 14240. If you live outside North America, check your local nursery, or write to Stokes for the name of a supplier in your area.

You can grow catnip indoors or outdoors, but outdoors is better. I have no luck with indoor plants, as Dayoh rips them out of the pots and stashes them under the chesterfield. For a good-looking bumper crop, remember to keep cutting back the tops of the plants so they will stay nice & bushy. If you don't, they will soon look scraggly and pathetic.

Nurseries and plant places sometimes sell catnip in little pots in the herb section. If you want a good crop of leaves, transplant the wee plant to a bigger pot. Catnip in pots does best in cool, moist, sunny surroundings, so if you're a city person it will probably do better on your balcony than inside your house or apartment.

STORING CATNIP

Freezing is my number one choice, as frozen catnip is almost as good as fresh. Save some plastic containers from yogurt, sour cream, etc., and wash them out really good. On the lid put a label that says Catnip and the date.

Don't bother washing the leaves. Just strip the leaves from the stalks (save the stalks for drying and stuffing toys) and pack the leaves into the container, topping it off with a piece of plastic wrap or waxed paper, then your lid with the date. Put the container in the freezer.

If you have a big crop, you can fill up a couple of containers in no time. If you have a small amount, pack fresh leaves into the container, cover with paper and put in the freezer, adding more leaves to the container as they appear.

To dry catnip for toys, tie a nice piece of string or yarn around a freshly picked bunch and hang it upside down from a hook, curtain rod, light fixture or whatever for a month or two until it's dry. Choose the right place in your porch or kitchen, and it will look like something out of one of those fancy decorating magazines. When dry, strip the leaves and flowers from the plants and store in a pretty jar with a screw-top. I leave mine right out on the kitchen counter next to my canisters.

CATNIP PARTY

On miserable days when we're down in the dumps, I take a handful of leaves out of the freezer. By the time I get to the cats, the leaves are almost defrosted. Then I sit on the floor and rip one leaf apart at a time and hold it up so kitty can rub her nose and cheeks across it before snapping it down. Sometimes I have a leaf or two myself.

Warning: Don't let your little friends o.d. on the weed! Cats who are overexposed to catnip can become bored with it, which is sad indeed. It's not the amount of catnip that's the problem, but the frequency of exposure, so keep those catnip parties down to one or two a month.

4
TOYS & STUFF

Happy toy-making, my friend. No matter how your toys turn out, kitty will love every one of them because they smell like you and not Korea. Most of my toys are so easy to make, you can probably start right away from things that you already have hanging around the house. You don't have to be a genius with a needle, you don't need a sewing machine, an ironing board or any fancy-shmancy equipment or skills. Even Brownies who failed darning can whip up these one-of-a-kind toys in no time flat. And the knitting stitches are so easy, I bet a friend could teach you all you need to know over a cup of tea. So don't be afraid. Not even you guys! I know several manly men who knit.

First, you should start saving all these nifty cat-toy-makings that you have probably been throwing out in the trash.

- Paper bags (all kinds & sizes).
- String, twine & ribbon from packages.
- Corks from wine bottles.
- Pretty scraps of fabric (avoid fuzzy).
- Shoeboxes.
- Ends of knitting yarn.
- Crinkly cellophane from tea & biscuit boxes, cigarette packs, etc.
- Wide elastic bands that come wrapped around broccoli.
- Tissue paper (save this from gifts or packages from fancy stores).
- Twist ties.
- Pistachio shells (nothing else makes quite as cute a clickety-click as these kitty-cat castanets).
- Old pantyhose & socks.
- Nice paper of any kind (not newspaper, which is dirty, smelly & wimpy).

Put all of these things in a special drawer or shopping bag. Then you won't have to search around every time you want to make a toy.

All the other materials for my cat toys are pretty standard and can be bought at most craft stores or notions departments.

Always use cotton or cotton blend yarn for the knitted toys. They will look wonderful, they will move & bend freely, and they will be user-friendly to puss's finely tuned senses. Don't even think of using Sayelle or the like, or the toys will turn out like loggy blobs.

Here's the thickness of yarn I like:

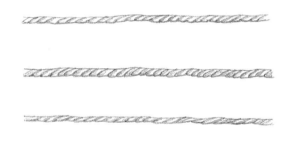

Plain old string is also the right weight, if you don't mind albino toys! All my knitted toys can be made with Metric 3.5 mm/U.S. 4 knitting needles.

Don't be tempted to use small buttons, sequins or craft-store glass eyes for toys, as they can easily come off and be swallowed or choked on by puss. Instead, embroider little eyes, noses & mouths using a simple satin stitch as shown here. Don't be afraid to try this simple stitch. My embroidering is really clunky, but this helps give each face I make a very personal, dopey look that is much better than a lot of too-cute clones:

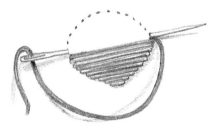

I use a simple backstitch for all seams, as it is stronger than a running stitch:

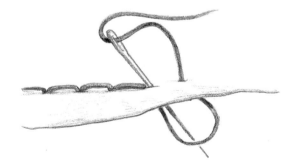

The Important Art of Stuffing

Each pattern that calls for stuffing gives you amounts to use, but it's best to judge for yourself so your toys will be just right—nice and tossable and with just the right irresistible sound.

Here are some things to remember:

- Never overstuff a toy, or it won't look, feel or move properly.
- Listen to the sound of the stuffing by jiggling it back & forth in the toy before you sew the final seam. If the stuffing doesn't move around and make the most thrilling little hisssshhing sound, the toy is overstuffed.

- The lighter the weight of the toy, the more flexible & flingable it will be, so don't overdo it on the beans.
- Supermarket catnip is fine for stuffing toys, but homegrown dried stuff is dynamite (see Chapter 3).

The Toy Box

Maybe you have a nice basket that's done nothing more useful than collect dust. Wouldn't it make an excellent toy box for kitty's precious stash? Put it on the floor in a spot where it looks attractive and is handy for your pal. Now puss can help himself whenever he's in the mood. And if you can teach him to put his toys away, you're a genius!

Two Cute Fishies

What cat wouldn't love to have some raunchy knitted fishies to call his own. These are such cuties that I knit schools of them for my darlings and as gifts for friends who have cats. They would also make super-duper craft items for the church bazaar. Put three in a nice greeting card box lined with tissue paper. Charge a lot, and I'll bet you get it.

Sonia Sunfish (Very Easy)

Little Sonia here is so simple, you can make a whole one while watching Dallas.

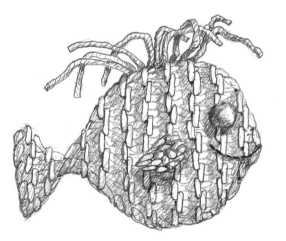

What You Need

- A small amount of cotton yarn. I used a soft yellow to make mine, but any fine- to medium-weight cotton or cotton blend will do (see yarn guide on page 58).
- Knitting needles (Metric 3.5 mm/U.S. 4).
- Stuffing ingredients: 1 large dried lima bean, 4 half pistachio shells (from 2 whole pistachios), 3 dried kidney beans, 2 pinches of barley and a spoonful of dried catnip.
- Darning needle.
- Two tiny 1/4-inch (5 mm) pompoms (sold in 25-packs at craft stores).
- A regular needle with thread to match the pompoms.

How to Make It

BODY

Tail side:
Cast on 2 stitches
Row 1: Inc 1 in each stitch
Row 2: Inc 1, K2, inc 1
Row 3: Inc 1, K4, inc 1
Row 4: Inc 1, K6, inc 1
Row 5: Inc 1, K8, inc 1 (12 stitches)
Rows 6 to 15: K across
Row 16: K2tog, K8, K2tog

Row 17: K across
Row 18: K2tog, K6, K2tog
Rows 19 & 20: K across
Row 21: K2tog, K4, K2tog
Row 22: K across
Row 23: K2tog, K2, K2tog
Row 24: K across
Row 25: K2tog twice
Row 26: K across
Row 27: Inc 1 in each stitch (4 stitches)
Row 28: K across
Row 29: Inc 1, K2, inc 1
Rows 30 & 31: K across and cast off

Other side:
Work the same as tail side to the end of
    Row 25
Row 26: K2tog & tie off

FINS (Make 2):

Cast on 1 stitch
Row 1: Inc 1
Row 2: Inc 1 in each stitch (4 stitches)
Row 3: K across
Row 4: K2tog twice
Row 5: K2tog & tie off

To make up the fish, sew together the two sides, leaving a small opening for the stuffing. Add the stuffing and sew up the hole.

Cut 5 or 6 pieces of yarn about 3 inches (7.5 cm) long. One at a time, thread them on a darning needle and run them through the top of the fish to make a dorsal fin. When you have run each piece of yarn halfway through, remove the needle and secure the yarn with double knots. Repeat until you've got a good-looking fin.

Thread your regular needle with regular thread and sew the eyes onto the sides of the face good & tight.

Thread your darning needle with yarn and sew the little fins on each side of the body.

You can make a cute little satin-stitch mouth or a running-stitch smile for the bazaar fishies, but honestly, your cats couldn't care less.

Tweedie Trout (Easy Enough)

I didn't know how attractive a trout could be til I saw this one. Your cat will say, "Hi, Gorgeous," and be more than proud to hang around with such a handsome dude. Use a nice fishy tweed color.

What You Need

- A small amount of medium-weight (see page 58) cotton yarn, preferably tweed.
- Knitting needles (Metric 3.5 mm/U.S. 4).
- Darning needle.
- Contrasting yarn scraps for eyes.
- Stuffing ingredients: 1 big dried lima bean, 3 dried kidney beans, 6 dried black beans, 4 pinches of barley and a spoonful of dried catnip.

How to Make It

BODY

Cast on 2 stitches
Row 1: Inc 1 in each stitch (4 stitches)
Row 2: K across
Row 3: Inc 1, K2, inc 1 (6 stitches)
Row 4: K across
Row 5: Inc 1, K4, inc 1 (8 stitches)
Row 6: K across
Row 7: Inc 1, K6, inc 1 (10 stitches)
Row 8: K across
Row 9: Inc 1, K8, inc 1 (12 stitches)
Row 10: *K2, P2, repeat from * to end
Row 11: Inc 1, K1, P2, K2, P2, K2, P1, inc 1 (14 stitches)
Row 12: K3, P2, K2, P2, K2, P3
Row 13: Inc 1, K2, P2, K2, P2, K2, P2, inc 1 (16 stitches)
Row 14: *P2, K2, repeat from * to end

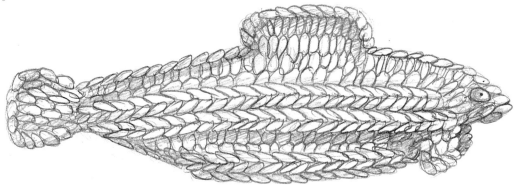

Row 15: Inc 1, P1, K2, P2, K2, P2, K2, P2, K1, inc 1 (18 stitches)

Rows 16 to 23: P3, *K2, P2, repeat from * to last 3 stitches, K3

Row 24: P2tog, P1, K2, P2, K2, P2, K2, P2, K1, K2tog

Rows 25 & 26: *P2, K2, repeat from * to end

Row 27: P2tog, K2, P2, K2, P2, K2, P2, K2tog

Row 28: P1, K2, P2, K2, P2, K2, P2, K1

Row 29: K2tog, K1, P2, K2, P2, K2, P1, P2tog

Row 30: *K2, P2, repeat from * to end

Row 31: K2tog, P2, K2, P2, K2, P2tog

Row 32: K1, P2, K2, P2, K2, P1

Row 33: P2tog, P1, K2, P2, K1, K2tog

Row 34: *P2, K2, repeat from * to end and cast off

TAIL

Cast on 4 stitches

Rows 1 to 6: K across and cast off

DORSAL FIN

Cast on 9 stitches

Row 1: *K1, P1, repeat from * to end

Row 2: K2tog, P1, K1, P1, K1, P1, K2tog and cast off

SIDE FINS (Make 2)

Cast on 1 stitch

Row 1: Inc 1

Row 2: Inc 1 in each stitch (4 stitches)

Row 3: K across

Row 4: K2tog twice

Row 5: K2tog & tie off

To make up the fish, with contrasting yarn, make two sly eyes close together at the front of the trout's face. This is done by repeating a simple backstitch (see page 58) about three times in the same spot.

Starting at his snout, sew up your trout to the end of his belly, leaving the end open for stuffing. Add the stuffing and finish sewing across the belly and the rear end.

Sew on the tail, then sew the fins on each side of the face. Sew the dorsal fin on top.

Is this a hunky-dory fish, or what?

Sock Ness Monster

At first I thought this wasn't going to be that good-looking a monster. Boy, was I fooled! DeeDee likes getting it in a clutch and kicking the daylights out of it with her back feet.

What You Need

- One green cotton knee sock with a nice ribbed or small woven pattern (these look like big fish scales). I was lucky enough to have such a knee sock already, but any old knee sock will do.
- One small metal jingle bell.
- Some pieces of yarn that match the sock color (more or less).
- Three heaping spoonfuls of dried catnip.
- Thread to match the sock.
- Needle.
- Scissors.
- Straight pins.
- Lots of crinkly cellophane and tissue paper (not as in toilet, but as in wrapping).

How to Make It

First cut off the ribbed top of the sock. Now cut the ribbed top up one side, then the other to give you two pieces that already look like fins. Keep one piece big and cut the other piece in half. Set aside.

This is the fun part! Start by shoving a piece of cellophane into the toe area of your sock. Listen to it hiss and make unearthly noises. Now, with a piece of yarn, tie this cellophane into the toe area to make what looks like that small head you saw in the pictures of the Loch Ness version. The yarn should only be tight enough to hold the head in place, not strangle it.

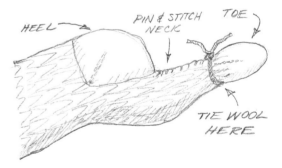

With a couple of straight pins, shape the long thin neck by pinning back the undersole of the sock from the back of the little head to the heel. Stitch the fold with your needle & thread and then remove the pins.

Here's where your monster starts looking like something! Using cellophane, stuff the neck and then the big hump and then the big body of the creature. The neck and hump should be pretty firm, but the body should be lightly packed so it can wiggle from side to side. (With an open-weave sock you see the cellophane glistening through just like fish scales.)

Now, throw the catnip into the tail end of the beast and shake it down into the sock. Tie off the tail end with yarn, onto which you've attached the jingle bell. The end of the sock will form a nice fish-type tail.

With your needle & thread, sew on the big fin at the top of the hump, just behind the heel. Make a pleat in each of the little fins by running your thread through them, then attach one to each side of the sock right where the heel stitching ends.

All your monster needs now is some beady little embroidered eyes and maybe a nice smile.

DUMDUM DOG

Dumdum dog is a meathead who comes from a bad home where he is not taught respect for felines and other people's property. Dumdum's owners deserve a good kick in the keester. As this is not possible without getting charged with assault, your cats can instead have this version of the dense and dreaded Dumdum to kick around and otherwise abuse.

If you and your felines have a real-life Dumdum in your neighborhood, use his given name or, for that matter, any rude name of your choice.

WHAT YOU NEED

- A long-sleeved fleece-lined sweatshirt. Here's your chance to get rid of that shirt that shrank or is getting ratty. If it has a stupid saying or a picture of a boogying beer bottle on it, all the better, as this is a dumb, dumb dog.
- Largish sheet of paper (for drawing the pattern) and pencil.
- Thread to match the sweatshirt.
- Scissors.
- Seam ripper.
- Needle and pins.
- Two big buttons for the eyes.
- Knitting needles (Metric 5 mm/U.S. 8).
- A small metal jingle bell.
- A small amount of chunky-weight yarn.

- Four pull-tabs from soda pop or beer cans (file the rough spots or cover them with three or four coats of nail polish).
- Tissue paper (not the kind you blow your nose in, but the crinkly wrapping type).
- A hankie-sized square (more or less) of crisp cello-wrap (the very crispy stuff that's wrapped around biscuit & tea-bag boxes, audio cassettes & records, Q-tips, cigarette packs—look around, you've got it).
- About 60 half pistachio shells (from 30 whole pistachios).
- A large, very crinkly cellophane potato chip bag (empty).
- Eight to ten beer caps.
- Two handfuls of dried catnip.
- One small dried pea for Dumdum's brain.

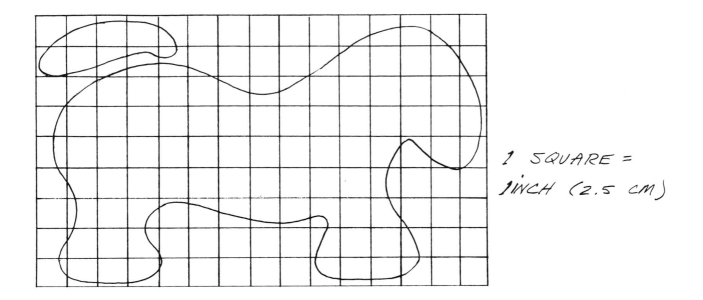

1 SQUARE =
1 INCH (2.5 CM)

HOW TO MAKE IT

On the piece of paper, copy the pattern of the body & tail.

Turn the sweatshirt inside out and pin the pattern to it. Cut out the pattern. Remove the pattern from the fabric and repin.

Remove the sleeve cuffs from the sweatshirt, using a seam ripper to do the job neatly and fast.

Stitch around the tail, leaving the bottom end open. Turn the tail right side out, using the end of a pencil if necessary to get into the corner and give it a wicked point.

Stuff the tail with the square of cello-wrap.

Then add about 6 half pistachio shells. Sew up the end so the stuffing doesn't fall out.

Insert the tail into the dog's hindquarters and pin it in place. The point of the tail can go up (for a cocky, smart-aleck jerk) or down (for a moody, miserable cur). Sew around the body, leaving the stomach open for the stuffing. Turn the body right side out.

Stuff the head with the tissue paper until it has a good shape, remembering to insert the tiny pea brain in one of the wads.

Next, stuff the feet with tissue, again packing it in for a decent shape.

Insert the potato-chip bag in the main section of the body, then add the remaining pistachio shells and the beer caps, pushing them into the back, front of the neck, tops of the legs, etc., so they'll be well spread out. Now dump in the catnip and sew up the stomach.

Sew on the two big button eyes very securely.

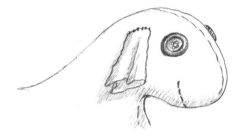

To make the ears, fold one cuff in half lengthwise and pin the unfinished edge in position on the dog's head. Now you've given him a good cuff in the ear. (Ha, ha, seamstress humor.)

As you sew on the ear, fold the unfinished edge under a bit to form a neat seam.

Now sew on the other ear. Pretty good ears, eh? And so easy.

Knit the dog collar by casting on 4 stitches, leaving a nice long tail on your yarn. Use a simple garter stitch (knit all stitches) til the collar measures about 10 inches (25 cm) long. Cast off, leaving a yarn tail about 6 inches (15 cm) long.

Insert two pull-tabs, then the jingle bell, then two more tabs on one of the long yarn ends, then tie with three or four strong knots. Cut off the extra yarn.

Place the collar around the dog's neck and sew up the end seam of the collar so the tabs dangle under the neck like dog tags.

Now . . . throw him to the cats!

They'll hate him to pieces.

CALHOUN CATERPILLAR

My sister Pearl thinks Calhoun looks more like a centipede than a caterpillar because of his many legs. Cats, on the other hand, are far too smart to involve themselves in such a discussion. One thing everyone will agree on — Calhoun really is cute.

WHAT YOU NEED

- One plastic hair roller with foam pad.
- Darning needle.
- Two 2-inch (5 cm) pieces of pipecleaner.
- Lots of yarn scraps about the length of your thumb.
- A small ball of yarn.

HOW TO MAKE IT

Remove the foam pad from the plastic roller. Thread the end of the yarn ball onto the darning needle and run it through the center hole of the foam pad. Remove the needle. Wrap the yarn round & round the foam to make a nice fat body, then tie the two ends nice & tight.

Put the roller back together again. The fastener end will be the face part because it looks like a nose. On each side of the nose, attach a pipecleaner by shoving it halfway through and giving it two twists. Eureka! A naked caterpillar with two fuzzy antennae.

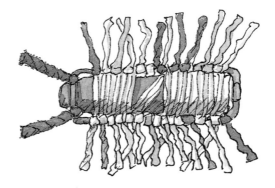

Now comes the fun part! Tie all those little yarn pieces onto the sides of the plastic roller and onto the yarn on the body part. Tie double knots so they stay put. The more yarn you put on, the cuter Calhoun gets.

If you really have your heart set on a centipede, tie yarn to the plastic sides only. Either way, this is fiddly work, so it's best to do it while you're watching TV. When your crawly critter looks just right, stop. Then start another one for your friend's cat, or make Calhoun a little brother or sister.

DELORES MOUSE

A beautiful mouse like this should have a beautiful name, so I called her Delores after my great-aunt. Every mouse comes out different, so you should name yours what you like. (If it comes out ugly, call it Quasimodo.)

WHAT YOU NEED

- A small amount of nice light- to medium-weight cotton yarn (see page 58) in white, gray, brown, tweed or mouse color of your choice.
- Knitting needles (Metric 3.5 mm/U.S. 4).
- Stuffing ingredients: 2 peanuts, 4 pistachio nuts, a small piece of cellophane that makes a crinkly sound, a heaping spoonful of catnip.
- Darning needle.
- Regular needle.
- A bit of contrasting yarn for the eyes.
- Three pieces of black thread, each about 12 inches (30 cm) long.

HOW TO MAKE IT

BODY

Cast on 25 stitches, leaving a long piece of yarn at the end of the row (this will be the tail)

Rows 1 to 16: K across—you should have about 1 1/2 inches (3.75 cm)

Row 17: *K3, K2tog, repeat from * to end (20 stitches)

Rows 18 to 20: K across

Row 21: *K2, K2tog, repeat from * to end (15 stitches)

Rows 22 to 24: K across

Row 25: *K2, K2tog, repeat from * to last stitch, K1 (12 stitches)
Rows 26 to 28: K across
Row 29: *K2, K2tog, repeat from * to end (9 stitches)
Row 30: K across
Row 31: *K1, K2tog, repeat from * to last stitch, K1 (6 stitches)
Row 32: K across
Row 33: K2tog to end and cut yarn to about 4 inches (10 cm); thread darning needle and draw yarn through 3 stitches on knitting needle and tie off

EARS (Make 2)

Cast on 3 stitches
Rows 1 to 4: K across
Row 5: Sl 1, K1, psso, K1
Row 6: Sl 1, K1, psso and tie off

Fold the body in half lengthwise and sew up, leaving the rear end open.

Make whiskers by running the black thread doubled through the nose area. Tie in three good-looking nose-like knots.

Give your mouse two nice eyes by making three big French knots a bit above the nose. Sew the ears above the eyes.

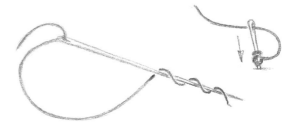

Add the stuffing. Depending on how big your mouse came out, you could use a nut or two more or less. When stuffed, the mouse should have a nice shape, but not be so packed that the thingamajigs inside can't move around and make those magic mousy sounds.

Sew up the rear end and trim the tail to a perfect length (too long is better than too short).

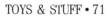

THREE BAGS FULL

All cats love paper bags, so even unfilled they're great toys. But think how much more exciting a bag can be with some of your baby's favorite things inside. Whoopee! So start saving your paper bags—bag toys don't last very long, but what does it matter when the bags are free and the toys are so easy to make.

GROCERY BAG TOY

This is made from—what else?—a big brown bag from the grocery store.

Open the bag as wide as it can go and put a few of pussum's favorite things inside— maybe a foilball (see page 14), a few broccoli bands, a biff bag (see page 78), whatever. Some pusses like to pretend the bag is a tent and stay inside with their toys scouting people they can pounce on. This is even more fun if you have two cats, because then they can pounce on each other.

LIQUOR STORE BAG TOY

First off, you need one of those long, thin, brown paper bags, so you're going to have to go to the liquor store and get yourself a nice bottle of wine. When you get home, pour yourself a big glass, then put the bag on the floor with something special inside it. How about a cat yummy? Puss will have a great time squeezing into the bag to get it. You'll have a great time watching. After your clever cat gets the first yummy, put in another. Maybe you'd like another glass of wine. Isn't this fun?

This toy works swell for kittens and thin cats who can squeeze into the bag. Dayoh is too big-boned to play, so he just watches. If your cat is pudgy, well, just roll the bag into a nice ball and toss it around for him.

Bitsy Bag Toy

My Siamese baby girls, Sheena & Bambi, go bonkers over this swishy, delicious-smelling toy.

You make this toy from a really small paper bag—like the kind you get when you buy nasal spray at the drugstore.

Put some noisy things into this little bag. Anything will do. I just opened one and found a Thank You Call Again receipt for $3.62, a piece of crinkly cellophane from those little packs of crackers, a cello-wrapped round chocolate mint candy, and that magical ingredient, catnip—a spoonful will do.

When you have filled your bitsy bag with interesting thingamabobs, throw in the catnip, give the top of the bag a twist, then wrap a thin elastic band* around it nice & tight. With a small skewer or darning needle, prick the bag about six times. Toss the bitsy bag on the floor, and it's rock & roll time. When the bag gets ripped up, make another.

---

* Some cats think thin elastic bands are chewing gum, so I don't use them in any toy where they might come loose. In this case they're fine.

Paper Toys

Even a bumbler can be an expert toymaker with paper toys. Roll a piece of paper into a nice tight ball. Toss it to your sweetie. Congratulations! You've made your first paper toy. However you rolled it, you can't go wrong, because cats love paper. When the toy has been loved to pieces, a new paper toy can be made in seconds, or a few minutes, tops.

Balls

Balls are best made from good-quality paper, as these throw better and are less offensive to puss than newsprint. Now you know what God made memos from the boss for! Paper bags are also excellent, as they give your ball-player a variety of sizes to play with, according to her game of the moment.

Bows & Butterflies

I make these feline faves from all my losing lottery tickets. You make the bow by twisting the ticket a few times in the middle so it forms a bow. A bow becomes a butterfly by wrapping a twist tie from a sandwich bag around the middle to form cute little antennae. All my babes love carrying around butterflies just like they're the real thing.

DANGLERS

These are just pieces of paper twisted in the middle and secured with a long string, then dangled for puss to bat at.

Use one sheet of paper and cut into the ends on each side to form fringes that rustle when batted. Use cellophane for a lighter, prettier, crispier dangler.

You can personally hold danglers for kitty to jump for or bat at, or you can hang them from a doorknob, the back of a chair or the chandelier. Best of all, hang one from the curtain rod in front of an open window. This is very bonny in cellophane with a nice long piece of yarn or ribbon that matches your drapes.

PIPECLEANER TOYS

Cats love pipecleaners almost as much as paper bags. They will have a ball with even a grotty old twist tie, so you could say the pipecleaner is the Cadillac of twist ties. When you take the time to make something special out of pipecleaners, pussum will love them even more. Here are two of our faves.

OLYMPIC RINGS (Makes 2 sets)

This toy is a real winner—easy to make, beautiful to look at and great for your little athlete to parade around with and show off her gymnastic grace. If you like, just for a little joke, you can make up a card with a perfect 10 on it and hold it up for kitty to see after her performance.

WHAT YOU NEED

• Five pipecleaners, each about 12 inches (30 cm) long (one each of red, blue, green, black & yellow). Buy these in the mixed colored pack and you'll get all of these and many more colors.
• Scissors.

HOW TO MAKE IT

Cut each pipecleaner in half. Now you'll have ten pieces, enough for two sets of rings.

Form the Olympic rings by turning each piece into a perfect O, starting with the black pipecleaner and looping through the others in the following order: blue, green, red, yellow. Now they're official! (For people who say cats are color-blind so what does the order of the colors matter, I can say only this: Be a class act and do it right!)

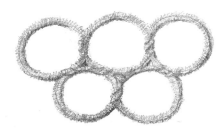

PRETZELS

Pretzels are very jolly-looking, and I like them a lot. They're not bad with a nice brewskie, either. Sometimes I find pipecleaner pretzels in my bed when I get up in the morning. I start the day with a smile and no crumbs.

WHAT YOU NEED

• One 12-inch (30 cm) brown or pretzel-colored pipecleaner.

HOW TO MAKE IT

If you've ever made pretzels, you already know how to shape this. If not, here's how:

Curve the pipecleaner into a horseshoe shape with the ends pointing toward you (1). Cross the ends over each other and twist (2).

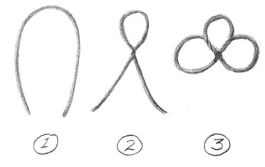

Then twist one end around the left side and one around the right side to form a perfect pretzel shape, and tuck the ends into the top loop (3). Cute, eh?

Gordie Garter Snake

Gordie is so adorable, I just let him lie around wherever the cats leave him. He really adds a cute and casual touch to any piece of furniture or any corner of any room. Your regulation garter snake in size, he's bendy, hissy and jingly to boot. The tweed yarn also makes him mossy, scaly and as handsome a reptile as you'd ever want to meet.

What You Need

- Knitting needles (Metric 3.5 mm/U.S. 4).
- A small amount of light- to medium-weight tweed yarn (see page 58).
- One small metal jingle bell.
- Two spoonfuls of dried catnip.
- A small amount of crinkly cellophane.
- Small scraps of yarn for the eyes and tongue.
- Darning needle.

How to Make It

Cast on about 100 stitches. Work about 16 rows of garter stitch (K, K, K, K, etc.) and cast off.

Sew across one end and about 1 1/2 inches (3.75 cm) down the seam. Turn this section inside out and insert the jingle bell. This is Gordie's head. Isn't it perfect?

Now sew up the remaining opening about 2 inches (5 cm) at a time. First insert a bit of cellophane, then sew a bit, insert a bit of catnip, sew another bit, etc. Use the end of a pencil or knitting needle to push the stuffing in, but leave it loose and not packed tight. It's important to use only small amounts of stuffing, as it's more for sound, smell & feel than for shape. Too much stuffing and you'll have Gordie the stiff instead of the loose, swishy guy he's meant to be. When he's all filled, sew across the end to close him off.

To make the tail, get a longish piece of matching yarn and wrap it tightly around &

around the tail end from the tip to about 2 inches (5 cm) up the back. Tie it very tightly.

Lie your snake on his tummy with the seam at the bottom. Now look at the head part, and right where the tongue should be, insert a short piece of red, yellow or other snake-tongue-colored yarn of your choice with a darning needle. Pull the yarn through until the ends are even. Tie two tight knots to hold the tongue in place. If you want a shorter tongue, trim it.

Above the tongue, make two nice beady eyes. I just make a big knot in my yarn, run it into the place where one eye should be and out the other side where the other eye should be. Tie a big knot in this end and trim the yarn.

When your cat sees, hears & smells this snake, he'll like him better than the real thing.

Biff Bags

Biff bags can be made from just about any fabric or yarn that isn't fuzzy. Who said all those nice fabric scraps, bits of yarn and stuff from your rag bag wouldn't come in handy? The two secrets of a good biff bag are as follows—they must be small, and the stuff inside must be able to move about freely so when kitty gets ready to fling her biff with a sharp snap of her neck, it will go flying across the room to the most interesting places—sometimes on the coffee table, in the book case, on the rocking chair—a good biff can end up anywhere! Once DeeDee tossed one right into my cup of tea, amazing us all. A first-rate biff should make a hishing sound when picked up, and a cute clickety-thump when it lands.

Knitted Biff (Make 2)

What You Need

- A small amount of any kind of yarn that is lightweight and not fuzzy.
- Knitting needles in a weight to match the yarn (more or less).
- A darning needle.
- Stuffing ingredients: 3 dried lima beans, 4 dried kidney beans, 6 half shells from 3 pistachio nuts, a few pinches of barley and a spoonful of dried catnip.

How to Make It

Cast on 16 stitches. Work garter stitch (K,K,K,K, etc.) for about 25 rows, or until you have a 3-inch (7.5 cm) square. Cast off. Make your second square.

With a darning needle, sew up three sides, add the stuffing and sew the end to close. Nothing to it!

Hints & Variations

Lightweight to medium cotton or cotton-blend yarn makes the best biffs. For special occasions, gifts, or to sell at the church bazaar, you can cuten the basic biff with stripes, ribbed or seed stitch or tiny cable stitch. Or how about knitting one side and making the other from a nice coordinating scrap of fabric you've saved for just such an occasion? Make the biffs to match your decor so they'll always add a complimentary touch no matter where they land.

PANTYHOSE BIFF (Makes 2)

So easy to make from the toes of your old pantyhose. Give them a good wash first so puss doesn't make that funny face with an open mouth, muttering "yuck" under her breath!

WHAT YOU NEED

- Pair of old pantyhose.
- Two short pieces of string or yarn.
- Stuffing ingredients, per biff: 2 dried lima beans, 3 dried kidney beans, a spoonful of dried catnip, 8 half shells from 4 pistachio nuts.

HOW TO MAKE IT

Cut off the feet of the pantyhose. Fill with the stuffing ingredients. Tie yarn around the feet at about the halfway point so the stuffing has lots of room to swish around, and you have a nice tail on the end. Tie at least three knots to make sure the stuffing stays put. If you like, cut into the end section in four or five places to make a fringe. That's it. Talk about simple!

Kitten Mitten Biff

So pretty. So witty. I made lots from the sleeves of my old flannelette nightie. Make two mittens and sew one on each end of a piece of yarn or ribbon, and sell them at the church bazaar for a big profit.

What You Need

- Small scraps of nice friendly fabric — flannelette or cotton are my favorites.
- Tracing paper and pencil.
- Sewing needle.
- Straight pins.
- Thread to match the fabric.
- Scissors.
- Yarn or ribbon about 10 inches (25 cm) long (if you want to do the set for around the neck).
- Stuffing ingredients: 1 dried lima bean, 3 dried kidney beans, a spoonful of dried catnip, 2 pinches of barley.

How to Make It

With a piece of tracing paper, trace out the pattern. Cut out your pattern and pin it to two pieces of fabric, with the right sides of the fabric facing each other.

STITCHING LINE

Cut around the pattern, remove the pattern and pin the two pieces of fabric together again. Backstitch around the mitten (see page 58), leaving the bottom open.

Turn the mitten right side out. If need be, push out the thumb with the end of a pencil. Stuff and sew across the bottom to close. Cute, eh? If I were you I'd make lots of these, as you know how kittens like to lose their mittens!

Piñata

Your cat doesn't have to be Mexican to know what to do with a piñata. Donna and the little Siamese girls jumped for joy at the sight of this far-out goose piñata filled with catnip, cat treats and small individual gifts for each cat: for Donna, some fancy feathers from the notions section of a fabric store; for DeeDee, a new biff with a tiny jingle bell inside; for Dayoh, a new pipecleaner pretzel; for Sheena, some cellophane butterflies, and for Bambi, a velour powder puff from the drugstore.

When filling your piñata, remember to include at least one large spoonful of catnip and some cat yummies to give it a good smell.

Also make sure the little gifts are lightweight so the piñata moves about when batted.

Traditionally the piñata is a toy enjoyed by Mexican cats at Christmastime, as they have no Santa Claws. But regardless of your cat's background, she will enjoy this wonderful toy at Christmas, for her birthday or any special occasion.

You can fancy-up the goose piñata by using colored bags and colored paper for the bill & wings. This one is just made of plain old brown paper supermarket bags and leftover house-hold paper, and it's still gorgeous. The directions may seem long, but it only took me fifteen minutes to make mine, and that was with the little girls helping me.

What You Need

- One heavy brown paper bag about 8 inches (20 cm) wide and 16 inches (40 cm) long.
- One smaller paper bag about 4 inches (10 cm) wide and 10 inches (25 cm) long.
- Enough bright ribbon to make a nice bow.
- A medium-weight elastic band
- One cardboard roll from inside the toilet paper.
- A piece of office-size paper.
- A wad of tissue paper.
- A long piece of string or yarn for hanging the piñata.
- A marker pen for drawing the eyes and nose holes.
- Scissors.
- Glue.
- A skewer or knitting needle for making the holes.
- Cat treats and dried catnip.

How to Make It

Take the wad of tissue paper and stuff it into the smaller paper bag to form the goose's head. Make the neck by squeezing the bottom part of the bag right up to the head.

With scissors, make a slit in the natural fold in the top section of the big bag, as close to the sealed end as possible. Insert the head and neck into the opening.

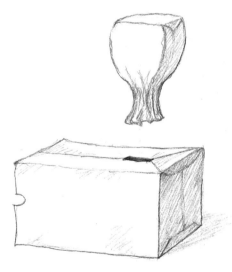

With scissors, cut four small slits in the big bag—two at the front of the neck and two at the back of the neck. Run the ribbon through the slits and tie in a nice big bow at the front.

cut ends meet. Cut this in half widthwise. Trace a bill pattern on one of the halves, keeping the rounded part of the bill at the uncut end of the cardboard.

Cut the sheet of paper in half widthwise. Make wings by folding each half, lengthwise, into accordion folds. Put a drop of glue between each fold, right at the end, so you have a fan. Then glue the fans on each side of the big bag to make wings. When the glue is dry, open the wing ends and fluff them out a bit.

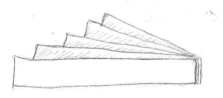

Make the beak by cutting down the side of the toilet paper roll and pressing it flat so the

With the marker, draw two nose holes just as on a real goose. Run some glue along the open edges of the beak and stick the beak right where it belongs on the goose's face.

Draw some goose-like eyes on the face. Can you believe how cute this is already?

Now take the catnip, treats & toys and put them in the big bag. Fasten the end with the elastic band, leaving a long tail. With scissors, cut the tail end in about five or six places to make a funky fringe.

With a skewer or knitting needle, punch

about twenty holes in the belly so the tempting aroma of all the special stuff inside can waft out.

About 2 inches (5 cm) behind the neck, make a hole and run the long piece of string or yarn through it so the goose is balanced when you dangle it.

Hang your piñata at a height your cats can reach when they stand on their tiptoes. If your cat is polite and well-mannered (unlike mine) and just sits there and sniffs and stares, give the piñata a little jiggle. Now kitty will know it's okay to bat at it, leap at it and rip it to shreds to get at the loot.

TRIXIE TOAD

Our backyard is full of darling little toads that I love & pamper almost as much as my cats. To make a long story short, most of my leggy-loves came from what used to be an empty lot next door with a natural spring, which I intended to buy and keep wild when I won the lottery. But wouldn't you know it? I still haven't won, and someone built a big house right on top of the spring and covered the rest of the yard with very boring grass. So all the toads moved to my yard, where all sorts of special things you hardly see anymore, including weeds, grow everywhere.

To make things perfect for my tiny refugees, I built some attractive toad condos from rocks hauled from the lake in the back of the Renault.

Our toad tribe is respected and admired by everyone except the kittens, who think they are tiny toys. Straight off, this rambunctious twosome was set straight on toad rights, and to keep them from terrorizing the wee ones, I made them some toads of their very own. Trixie and her brothers & sisters are equally adorable and, filled with catnip, they smell much better than frog flesh.

Use your best scraps for Trixie, as she's worth it. My Trixie is apricot with a pink & white flowered tummy, but a striped Trumbo, checked Treena, polka-dot Tilly and plaid Truman are just as wonderful. Whatever you do, remember to keep your tummy prints small, or your toads will look like they've been tattooed.

Toads are really fiddly to make, but turn out so sweet, I bet you'll end up making more than one.

WHAT YOU NEED

- Plain cotton scrap (for top) about 6 inches (15 cm) square.
- Coordinating printed cotton scrap for tummy, about the same size.
- Thread to match the plain scrap.
- Straight pins.
- Tracing paper.
- Needle.
- Pencil.
- Knitting needle.
- Two tiny 3/8-inch (9.5 mm) pompoms (sold in craft stores).
- Small funnel.
- Stuffing ingredients: a spoonful of dried catnip, a spoonful of barley, 6 half pistachio shells from 3 whole pistachios.

HOW TO MAKE IT

Trace out the toad pattern on your tracing paper and cut it out.

Pin the pattern to your two pieces of cotton (make sure the right sides of the material are facing each other).

STITCHING LINE

Cut around the pattern, remove the pattern, then pin the pieces together again.

Stitch around the toad with tiny fairy-like stitches (a backstitch is nice and strong, see page 58), leaving space between the legs for filling and turning.

Turn the toad right side out, using the end of a pencil to help push out the head, and the end of a knitting needle for the arms & legs. Work gently so you don't tear the seams.

Put the stuffing into the head & body area only, using the funnel for the catnip & barley. Insert the catnip first, then the pistachios. Add the barley last because you want most of the

pistachios to stay in the middle and the barley & catnip to move around.

Neatly stitch up the legs & crotch.

With your fingers, gently work a bit of the stuffing into the arms & legs.

Sew on one pompom eyeball and run the thread through the opposite side. Sew on the other pompom. Run the thread back & forth through the eyes to make them very secure.

Now sit Trixie up on her pert little tush and smile back at that adorable wee kisser. Maybe you'll want to keep her for yourself!

Spool Toys

Jingling, rolling, bumping, thumping — these clattering spool toys are rock 'n' roll music to your baby's perky ears. Fancy they're not, but they are funky and so easy to make from empty thread spools that would otherwise just end up in the landfill.

If you don't sew yourself, get friends who do to save their old spools for you. Like a wine cork, an empty spool will make old sweetie-face's day all on its own. Jazzed up, they're even more apt to amuse.

Mini Barbells

This can be a fairly quiet toy if you make it from Styrofoam spools. Some cats will be content to roll it around, but mainly I make these barbells for exhibitionists like Dayoh & Bambi, who love to carry things in their mouths while proudly cantering around on their longest legs.

What You Need

- One plastic drinking straw.
- Two matched 1-inch (2.5 cm) spools.
- Heavy-duty glue.

How to Make It

Run the straw through the spools so one spool sits on each end. Bend the ends of the straw back about 2 inches (5 cm) and give each end a good shot of glue. Shove the ends back into the spool holes, leaving about 1/4 inch (5 mm) or so sticking out each end.

Put the barbells in an out-of-the-way place until they are dry. Have you ever seen cuter barbells? I bet not! And after puss has pumped himself up a lot and the straw gets wrecked, all it takes is a few minutes to make a new set.

RUMBLE ROLLER

WHAT YOU NEED

- Three spools (all the same size).
- Two buttons (bigger than the holes in the spools, but smaller than the spool ends).
- About 12 inches (30 cm) heavy string or yarn.
- Darning needle.
- Scissors.

HOW TO MAKE IT

Thread your needle with the string and secure a button on the end. Add the three spools. Add the second button and secure it by running the string through the buttonhole, twisting it a few times around the base of the button, through the spools, around the other button, etc., until the string is short enough to tie in a final knot. All done. I told you it was easy to make, and not too noisy, as it just rumbles along ahead of pussy's power paw.

ROLLER JINGLE

WHAT YOU NEED

- One big spool — about 1 1/2 inches (3.75 cm) across the end is nice.
- Two small metal jingle bells.
- About 12 inches (30 cm) heavy string or yarn.
- Darning needle.
- Scissors.

HOW TO MAKE IT

Thread the needle with string and secure one jingle bell on the end. Add your big spool. Add your second jingle bell and secure it so the bells are tight on both ends by running the string back & forth through the spool, through the hole in the base of the bell, etc., until it's good & strong. Tie off and trim the string. Isn't it nifty? And it makes just the right amount of hubbub to excite your little friend, without giving you a headache.

CORKYPINE

This is a very scary critter. After one look and sniff at Corkypine, DeeDee's out to terminate it, and she does a pretty good job. I re-quill her Corkies so they can sometimes go two rounds. Donna just likes to slobber on hers and dance them around the floor a bit, so hers would last pretty well if her sister didn't demolish them.

WHAT YOU NEED

- One wine cork.
- A piece of yarn about as long as your forearm.
- Twelve to fifteen stems of dried catnip.
- Scissors.
- A marker pen for drawing the face.
- A big darning needle for punching holes.
- A thin but long darning needle (it must be longer than the cork, or forget it).
- Pliers with gripping teeth.
- A sharp knife.

HOW TO MAKE IT

With the sharp knife, cut on the diagonal (like for French-cut beans) a little hunk off the front of the cork. This will be the face part.

Thread the yarn onto the thin but long darning needle and make a nice big knot at the end. If you want a bigger nose, three or four knots would be better.

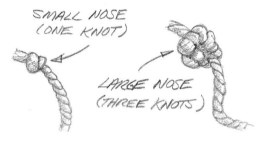

Now comes the hard part. Push the threaded needle through the bottom of the cork (on the face side), easing it through so you don't break the cork. When the tip of the needle pops through the rear end, use the pliers to pull it through. Now your Corkypine has a nose. Tie a whole bunch of knots in the rear end of the yarn, then cut it shorter or leave it longer for the tail of your choice.

Now comes the fun part. With the marker, draw on some eyes, a mouth and lots of dots around the nose. Or you can just give him a nice face like Uncle Louie.

With the big darning needle, carefully make a hole on Corky's back, then firmly but gently stuff it with a catnip quill, pushing the quill in as far as it will go. You'll get the hang of it after a few tries. Repeat about a dozen or so times until all the quills are stuffed.

If a quill breaks, pick it out with your needle and stuff the hole with another. Corkypines can be restuffed with new quills whenever they start looking ratty or start smelling boring. But when the cork starts going and won't hold quills, it's time for a trip to the wine store.

PANTYHOSE TOYS

An old pair of pantyhose and a few odds and ends are all it takes to make these four easy toys. Light, stretchy pantyhose, well laundered, of course, to remove exotic odors, make the perfect toys. They fly through the air so beautifully when kitty flings them. Stretchiness is a big bonus. When puss uses his mouth to help dislodge his entangled hooks, he often gets a challenging snap to his nose, which only makes the sport more interesting.

I made all four toys in one afternoon and had to sew the final seams standing in the middle of the room to keep my overly curious dearies from getting at the toys before they were finished.

TUG-OF-WAR AND JUMP ROPE

Make this toy first, as all you have to do is cut off one leg of the pantyhose right across the bottom of the hipline and give it a good stretch.

My cats like to play tug-of-war by grabbing one end of the leg in their mouths and trying to pull it away from me, which is great fun because of the stretchiness. When I let the kittens win, they run away with the rope for a victory romp through the house.

My Siamese cats love jumping for things, as did my part tabby-Siamese Pippin. To play jump rope, put a small pine cone, foilball (see page 14), walnut, or other small, light object into the toe of the rope and hold it up for puss to bat or jump at. The stretch and bounce will captivate kitty and give him a good workout.

CRINKLY CRACKER

Cute and easy to make, with a nice surprise inside, just like the party crackers people enjoy. Donna makes hers last for days, but Sheena & Bambi rip theirs apart in less than fifteen minutes.

WHAT YOU NEED

- Piece of pantyhose 5 inches (12 cm) long, from the leg section (without toe).
- A small piece of crinkly paper.
- A small spoonful of dried catnip.
- One cat yummy.
- Two plastic twist ties.

HOW TO MAKE IT

Wind one of the twist ties tightly around the pantyhose about 1 inch (2.5 cm) from one end. Fill the pantyhose with the crinkly paper, cat yummy and catnip. Close up the other end with the second twist tie. Now toss the cracker to your sweetie and watch her smile!

FUNKY BANANA

You make this from the stretchy cotton crotch, so you don't even need to cut a pattern. If your pantyhose is beige or brown, this will look like a real rotten banana, which will be even more lifelike than my mauve one. The heavy cotton makes this toy nice & sturdy.

Make up a whole bunch of funky bananas. Hang them on a nice piece of ribbon and display them at your next church bazaar. Cat lovers will snap them up!

WHAT YOU NEED

- Cotton crotch section from the pantyhose (I don't have to tell you that this should be well laundered with a heavy-duty detergent).
- Scissors.
- Thread.
- Needle.
- Pencil.

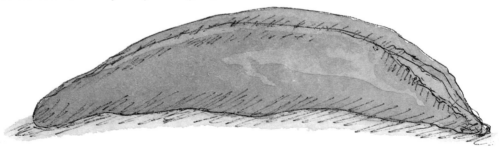

- Six half pistachio shells (from three whole pistachios).
- A small spoonful of dried catnip.

HOW TO MAKE IT

Very carefully cut the crotch section out of the pantyhose, making sure you don't cut too close to the seam that binds the cotton and pantyhose sections together. Fold the crotch in half lengthwise with the cotton on the outside. Doesn't it look like a banana already?

Stitch around the outside edge of your banana with a nice strong little backstitch, until you get about 2 inches (5 cm) from the end. Turn the banana right side out, using the pencil to push out the end.

Stuff the banana with the pistachio shells and catnip. Finish sewing up the open end, tucking in your edges for a neat finish.

Funky Worm

Half of a pantyhose waistband will make one excellent worm, so save the other half for a dear friend's cat. Unlike bananas, worms come in as many colors as pantyhose.

What You Need.

- Elastic waistband from pantyhose.
- Matching thread.
- Needle.
- Pencil.
- Small bit of contrasting yarn.
- Darning needle.
- Twelve half pistachio shells (from six whole pistachios).
- A big spoonful of dried catnip.

How to Make It

Very carefully cut the waistband away from the pantyhose, making sure you don't get too close to the seam, or your worm will run.

Cut the waistband in half at the side seams and set one aside.

With your regular needle and thread, sew across one end of the waistband. Then, with the help of your pencil, turn the waistband inside out. Stuff with two pistachio shells, a bit of catnip, two more shells, etc., until the whole worm is stuffed. It should be loose enough for everything to jiggle around inside.

Sew up the other end of the waistband.

Thread the darning needle with yarn. Make a big knot in one end and run the needle through one side of the worm's face and out the other. Tie another knot to form two big eyes. Repeat on the other end of the worm if you wish, as I believe worms have eyes on both ends, but I won't swear to it.

About the author

Helen Levchuk is a freelance writer who lives in Niagara-on-the-Lake, Ontario, with her daughter Alyson and an armload of cats. She has worked as a writer for Ogilvy & Mather and Vickers & Benson, and her work has won major advertising awards, including a Clio, Canadian and U.S. radio and TV awards, New York Art Director's Show award and a Billi for outdoor advertising. A long-time and passionate cat lover, she has worked extensively with a bevy of furry, four-legged experts on the toys and games that appear in this book.

About the illustrator

John Bianchi is a cartoonist, illustrator and author living near Bath in eastern Ontario. Twice nominated for Canada Council/Governor General's awards for his children's book illustrations, he is a winner of the New York Academy of Sciences' 1988 Children's Science Book Award. He is the author/illustrator of the Bungalo Boys books, as well as being the illustrator of *The Dingles*.

Many other fascinating books are available from Alaska Northwest Books.™ Ask at your favorite bookstore or write us for a free catalog.

Alaska Northwest Books™
A division of GTE Discovery Publications, Inc.

P.O. Box 3007
Bothell, WA 98041-3007
Call toll free 1-800-343-4567